Date: 7/26/18

J BIO BASTIAN
Felix, Rebecca,
Angie Bastian :
Boomchickapop boss /

Female FOODIES

Angie Bastian

BOOMCHICKAPOP Boss

Rebecca Felix

Checkerboard Library

An Imprint of Abdo Publishing
abdopublishing.com

abdopublishing.com

Published by Abdo Publishing, a division of ABDO, PO Box 398166, Minneapolis, Minnesota 55439. Copyright © 2018 by Abdo Consulting Group, Inc. International copyrights reserved in all countries. No part of this book may be reproduced in any form without written permission from the publisher. Checkerboard Library™ is a trademark and logo of Abdo Publishing.

Printed in the United States of America, North Mankato, Minnesota
102017
012018

THIS BOOK CONTAINS
RECYCLED MATERIALS

Design: Sarah DeYoung, Mighty Media, Inc.
Production: Mighty Media, Inc.
Editor: Liz Salzmann
Cover Photographs: Courtesy Angie Bastian, Shutterstock
Interior Photographs: Courtesy Angie Bastian, pp. 5, 7, 9, 11, 13, 15, 17, 19, 21, 23, 25, 28 (top, bottom), 29 (top, bottom)
Background Pattern: Shutterstock, cover, pp. 3, 5, 7, 9, 11, 13, 15, 17, 19, 21, 23, 25, 31

Publisher's Cataloging-in-Publication Data
Names: Felix, Rebecca, author.
Title: Angie Bastian: Boomchickapop boss / by Rebecca Felix.
Other titles: Boomchickapop boss
Description: Minneapolis, Minnesota : Abdo Publishing, 2018. | Series: Female foodies |
    Includes online resources and index.
Identifiers: LCCN 2017944036 | ISBN 9781532112645 (lib.bdg.) | ISBN 9781532150364 (ebook)
Subjects: LCSH: Bastian, Angela, 1960-.--Juvenile literature. | Businesswomen--United States--
    Biography--Juvenile literature. | Popcorn industry--Juvenile literature. | Entrepreneurship--Juvenile
    literature.
Classification: DDC 338.76647 [B]--dc23
LC record available at https://lccn.loc.gov/2017944036

Contents

Chapter 1

Popcorn Pioneer

You've just come home from school. You head to the kitchen for a snack. As you reach for the cupboard, you close your eyes and make a silent wish. You open the cupboard door, and it's there! Your dad remembered to restock your favorite flavor of BOOMCHICKAPOP. The entire bag of sweet and salty kettle corn is all yours!

BOOMCHICKAPOP is one of the top popcorn brands in the nation. The colorful bags and **unique** flavors make it a snack unlike anything else. Food company Angie's **Artisan** Treats owns the brand. The company operates giant factories in Minnesota and Nevada. But the first bags of Angie's popcorn were popped and packaged by hand.

Angie and Dan Bastian founded BOOMCHICKAPOP. The couple began the business in their Minnesota home. They made and bagged small batches of kettle corn in their garage and then sold the popcorn at local events. The Bastians named their snack after Angie. Almost immediately, their business took off! Today, Angie's name is found on **supermarket** shelves around the world.

Popcorn professionals call a popped kernel of popcorn a "flake."

Chapter 2

Indiana Upbringing

Angie Miller was born in Goshen, Indiana, on November 14, 1960. She has two younger brothers. Angie's father ran a **propane** gas company. It had offices in Goshen and in Sturgis, Michigan. The Millers lived in both towns during Angie's childhood. They moved to Sturgis when Angie was about two years old. The family returned to Goshen when she was ten years old.

Angie's grandfather lived in Goshen. The Millers built a home next door to his farm. Angie spent much of her time outdoors on the farm and its surrounding land. There, she would search for rocks and climb trees. She also loved reading, especially while outside. She also loved gymnastics, and was always practicing flips.

Angie was also assigned outdoor jobs as a child. Her father kept farm animals as a hobby, including

Food Bite

Angie's parents taught her that hard work was important. They believed that work came first and play came second.

From a young age, Angie learned about running a business from her father.

a few cows and chickens. Angie helped care for the animals. She helped her mother in the garden too.

Summers meant the end of the school year and more outdoor time for Angie. But she loved school so much that she was always sad when summer came. Her favorite subjects were English and history. Angie graduated from North Ridge High School in 1978.

Chapter 3

Career Moves

After high school, Miller worked for her father. He was running a **recreational vehicle** dealership. Miller took a job as the company secretary, earning $2 per hour.

During this time, Miller visited her aunt, Kristine Miller, in Colorado. Kristine was a nurse. She encouraged Miller to consider going to college. When Miller returned home, she entered the nursing program at Goshen College. After graduation, her career took her all over the country.

Miller's first nursing job was in Sarasota, Florida. Miller worked in Sarasota for a short time. She then worked in Ohio for a year. In 1989, Miller moved to Atlanta, Georgia, to continuing growing her nursing career and education. There, she attended Emory University, studying **psychiatric** nursing and **gerontology**. Miller graduated in 1991.

After graduation, Miller moved to Gallup, New Mexico. Gallup was a small town with a small hospital. Miller made friends with several hospital staff members. A connection made through these friendships would soon change Miller's life forever.

Miller quickly fell in love with nursing and helping people.

Chapter 4

Chance Meeting

While working in Gallup, Miller stayed very busy. She didn't always take care of her health. If Miller didn't drink enough water or get enough rest, she would sometimes faint. One summer day in 1992, she fainted in the hospital elevator. Miller broke her jaw in several places when she fell. It had to be wired shut for six weeks. After that time, a surgeon could operate to repair her jaw.

Miller was crushed. Her career was taking her to Wyoming next. She already had a job lined up there. But traveling with her injury would be difficult. Miller canceled her plans. She stayed in Gallup to rest and wait for surgery.

One day, Miller attended a gathering at the home of the hospital's **CFO**. Miller's wired jaw drew the immediate attention of the CFO's nephew, Dan Bastian. Dan was originally from Minnesota, where he had earned a history degree from St. John's University. As a college student, Dan had broken his jaw playing baseball for the St. John's team.

As an adult, Dan lived several places, working as a teacher. He taught English in Mexico and math in Belize. He

Miller always wants to improve. She once said, "Let's be the Wonder Woman of the snack shelf."

moved to New Mexico to be near extended family that lived there. Dan taught social studies and Spanish in New Mexico.

Like Dan, Miller had traveled many places. She had even been in Belize around the same time Dan was! Dan and Miller bonded over their shared experiences. They began dating.

Chapter 5

Family Life

Miller married Dan in 1994 and took his last name. The next year, they welcomed a daughter, Aunikah. Their son, Tripp, was born in 1997. The Bastians lived in Gallup for another year after his birth.

In 1998, the Bastians moved Santa Fe, New Mexico. The family lived there for a couple of years. They then moved to Sarasota, where Bastian's parents lived.

The family often visited Dan's home state of Minnesota. Bastian liked the people in Minnesota. She felt they were friendly and had a great sense of community. In 2001, the Bastians moved to North Mankato, Minnesota.

In Minnesota, Dan found work teaching and Bastian resumed her nursing career. They stayed very busy with work and raising their young children. The couple wanted to find a way to spend more time with one another and together as a family. They also wanted to earn more money to save for Aunikah and Tripp's college education.

Dan and Bastian began researching businesses **online**. They wanted to start a business while keeping their full-time

The Bastians enjoy family trips to places such as Whistler, Canada.

jobs. It needed to be a business the couple could run in the evenings and on weekends. They came across information about kettle corn. This is a sweet and salty popcorn traditionally made in cast-iron kettles.

People claimed to have made thousands of dollars making and selling kettle corn! The Bastians thought the recipe and process seemed simple enough. They bought a kettle, not knowing how much it would affect their lives.

Chapter 6

Home Business

Bastian and Dan got right to work when their kettle arrived in November 2001. They set up the 200-pound (91 kg) machine in their garage. The Bastians had received a basic recipe with their kettle purchase. Ingredients included popcorn **kernels**, oil, sugar, and salt.

The kettle was heated by an open flame. The Bastians burned the first couple batches of popcorn they made. But soon, they got the hang of it! They also began adjusting the recipe to add their own personal touches to it.

Bastian and Dan planned to sell their snack at local events and in store parking lots. Their first day of business was the day before Thanksgiving. The Bastians set up their tent outside the Rainbow Foods **supermarket** in the nearby city of Mankato, Minnesota. They knew the store would be busy with holiday shoppers.

Food Bite

With their kettle, the Bastians could make 300 bags of kettle corn in four hours!

One place the Bastians sold kettle corn was at home improvement store the Home Depot.

The couple had bagged popcorn ready to sell. But they also made popcorn on-site, hoping the smell of the snack popping would draw shoppers in. They were right! The Bastians sold small bags of kettle corn for $3 each and large bags for $5. They earned $300 total. The first day of Angie's Kettle Corn had been a success.

Chapter 7

Big Break

In the following months, the Bastians sold Angie's Kettle Corn at fairs, festivals, and other events. In summer 2002, one event brought the business its big break. The state's football team, the Minnesota Vikings, held a training camp in Mankato each summer. The camp lasted several days. Hundreds of people attended each day to watch the team practice.

Bastian and Dan set up their tent outside the training stadium, selling popcorn to fans. But then they got the idea for the players to try the kettle corn. Dan knew someone who was working with the Vikings staff that summer. Dan also knew that the team watched training videos together and held meetings.

Dan's contact agreed to let the Bastians give the team popcorn to eat during these gatherings. The Bastians packaged 120 bags

Food Bite

Aunikah and Tripp often joined their parents in the kettle corn tent.

The Bastians packaged their kettle corn in clear bags so Vikings fans could bring it into the stadium.

of popcorn for the Vikings players. The next morning, the Bastians learned the Vikings players, coaches, and staff had loved the popcorn!

In fact, the team liked it so much, it offered the Bastians a deal. Angie's Kettle Corn became the official kettle corn of the Minnesota Vikings. The company was given a space to sell kettle corn outside the stadium during every home game.

Chapter 8

Super Sales

Angie's Kettle Corn gained major exposure from the Vikings connection. The Bastians soon began selling it at other state sports events. This included Minnesota Timberwolves and Lynx basketball games and Minnesota Twins baseball games.

Word spread about the Bastians' popcorn. Grocery store managers began to take notice. In 2003, grocery store **chain** Lunds & Byerlys offered to sell Angie's Kettle Corn in its stores! Bastian and Dan were pleased. But they felt they weren't quite ready. They would need to make much larger quantities of kettle corn. The Bastians asked Lunds & Byerlys for more time to prepare for such a big change. The grocery store chain agreed.

Bastian and Dan found a commercial kitchen for rent inside a local bakery. They set up shop and got busy making popcorn. They

Food Bite

The bags of Angie's Kettle Corn sold in stores had **nutritional** information, **UPC codes**, and more printed on them.

Angie's BOOMCHICKAPOP is the official kettle corn of the Minnesota Twins.

also had new bags designed. Finally, the product was ready for store shelves. In May 2004, Angie's Kettle Corn made its first appearance in stores. It was sold at two Mankato Lunds & Byerlys **supermarkets** and in a nearby food co-op.

Around this time, Dan quit his teaching job. He would focus on the popcorn business full time. Bastian continued her nursing job. But she remained a vital force behind the business that bore her name.

Chapter 9

BOOMCHICKAPOP

Angie's Kettle Corn was an instant success. However, the Bastians did not advertise their product. Instead, they believed people would buy their popcorn if they tried it. So, Bastian and Dan gave away samples at **supermarkets**.

As more people tasted Angie's Kettle Corn, sales soared. The company needed more space for production. In 2007, Angie's Kettle Corn moved into a 20,000-square-foot (1,858 sq m) building in North Mankato. It allowed the company to pop enough corn to meet demand.

By 2010, Angie's Kettle Corn was in stores across the nation. As their business expanded, the Bastians often received requests from store managers. A common request was for other flavors of popcorn in addition to kettle corn.

Bastian and Dan had a decision to make. Their brand was called Angie's Kettle Corn. So, they could keep the name and make only kettle corn. Or, they could branch out and try new flavors. At the end of 2011, the Bastians began rebranding their business. The idea for Angie's BOOMCHICKAPOP was born.

In 2010, Bastian quit nursing to manage Angie's Kettle Corn full time.

Chapter 10

Fancy Flavors

The change from Angie's Kettle Corn to Angie's BOOMCHICKAPOP took time. By 2011, the company employed more than 150 people. Bastian and her staff came up with new flavor ideas. A team of **marketers** and designers created new bags. The bags had bright and pastel colors. BOOMCHICKAPOP was in large, bold letters.

Bright yellow bags of Sea Salt BOOMCHICKAPOP appeared in stores in May 2012. Within four months, the flavor overtook kettle corn as the company's best seller. In the following years, more BOOMCHICKAPOP flavors hit the shelves. These included Chocolate Drizzle, Sweet & Spicy, and special **seasonal** flavors. Each flavor is made from the same yellow corn grown in the Midwest. The company uses all-natural popcorn **kernels**, oils, and flavor ingredients.

Food Bite

In 2011, the Bastians appeared on the *Martha Stewart Show*. They taught Stewart how to make kettle corn.

Bastian's favorite
BOOMCHICKAPOP
flavor is Sea Salt.

Today, a professional research and development team invents new flavors. But Bastian still approves all of them. She tries them in the company's test kitchen in downtown Minneapolis, Minnesota.

Chapter 11

Keeping the Balance

By 2013, Bastian and Dan were very busy running their booming business! However, they made sure to keep their lives balanced. Spending time with Aunikah and Tripp is very important to Bastian and Dan. They are very proud that no matter how big BOOMCHICKAPOP got, the couple remained attentive parents.

Bastian and Dan also agreed on management styles. Bastian believes being a good leader means hiring good people and then standing back and letting them thrive. As BOOMCHICKAPOP continued to grow, Bastian and Dan realized they needed to follow this advice. They felt it would allow the company to continue expanding. Also, it would give them more time to stay well-connected to their children.

In 2014, the Bastians sold most of the company to private equity company TPG Growth. Three

Food Bite

✕

In 2015, BOOMCHICKAPOP opened a second production factory. It is in Reno, Nevada.

Bastian and some of the BOOMCHICKAPOP team were featured on the June 2014 issue of *Food Processing* magazine.

years later, US food manufacturer Conagra Brands Inc. bought Angie's Artisan treats. Bastian felt that Conagra would be able to satisfy customers' requests for more BOOMCHICKAPOP flavors in more stores. She assured fans that Angie's would continue to produce "snacks that you can feel good about feeding your family."

Chapter 12

Female Leader

At first, the Bastians didn't realize what a strongly female-oriented brand they were creating. **Marketing** research later showed them that women were the main BOOMCHICKAPOP buyers. Bastian decided she wanted her brand to influence these buyers positively.

One way the company does this is through its Crush It campaign. This campaign celebrates the way women **excel** in life, or "crush it," each day. This can include anything, from being a kind person to accomplishing a goal and more.

As part of the Crush It campaign, Bastian began the POP of Positivity Tour in 2017. Bastian and others from the company traveled the country. They shared **social media** videos of women explaining how they crush it. For Bastian, her popcorn is a way to spread this message of positivity.

For many satisfied customers, the Crush It campaign has taken on a second meaning. They share photos of themselves with an empty BOOMCHICKAPOP bag they've just "crushed," or eaten all of. The next time you crush one, think of Bastian and her brand's positivity!

Angie Bastian

By the Numbers

14

number of year-round
BOOMCHICKAPOP flavors

280

number of
BOOMCHICKAPOP
employees as of 2017

450-500

temperature in degrees
Fahrenheit (232-260°C)
at which popcorn pops

5,000,000

weight in pounds
(2,268,000 kg) each of
sunflower oil and cane
sugar BOOMCHICKAPOP
uses per year

20,000,000

weight in pounds
(9,000,000 kg) of popcorn
kernels BOOMCHICKAPOP
uses per year

25,000,000

number of bags of
BOOMCHICKAPOP sold
in 2017

Timeline

1960

Angie Miller is born on November 14 in Goshen, Indiana.

1978

Angie graduates from North Ridge High School. She gets a job at her father's recreational vehicle dealership.

2001

The Bastians move to North Mankato, Minnesota. They buy a kettle and start selling Angie's Kettle Corn.

2002

Angie's Kettle Corn becomes the official kettle corn of the Minnesota Vikings.

2012

The Bastians start making other flavors of popcorn and change the name to Angie's BOOMCHICKAPOP.

1991

Miller graduates from Emory University in Atlanta, Georgia. She moves to Gallup, New Mexico.

1994

Miller marries Dan Bastian and takes his last name.

2004

Angie's Kettle Corn starts being sold in stores.

2010

Bastian quits nursing to work at the company full time.

2014

The Bastians sell most of the company to TPG Growth.

2017

Bastian travels the country on the POP of Positivity Tour. Conagra Brands Inc. buys Angie's Artisan Treats.

Glossary

artisan – made by a person or company that produces something in limited quantities, often using traditional methods.

CFO – a chief financial officer. The CFO is the person in charge of the money received and spent by a company.

chain – a group of businesses usually under a single ownership, management, or control.

excel – to be better than others.

gerontology – the scientific study of old age and of the process of becoming old.

kernel – a whole seed of a grain, such as corn.

marketing – the process of advertising or promoting an item for sale. Someone who does this is a marketer.

nutritional – related to the vitamins, minerals, and other content of a food product.

online – connected to the Internet.

propane – a colorless gas that is used for cooking and heating.

psychiatric – of or relating to a branch of medicine focusing on mental, emotional, or behavioral health.

recreational vehicle – a vehicle designed for recreational use, such as camping.

seasonal – only available at certain times of the year.

social media – websites or smartphone apps that provide information and entertainment and allow people to communicate with each other. Facebook and Twitter are examples of social media.

supermarket – a large store that sells foods and household items.

unique (yoo-NEEK) – being the only one of its kind.

UPC code – *UPC* stands for universal product code. It is a series of black and white lines found on most products for sale. Each product has its own code, which is used to track sales.

Online Resources

Booklinks
NONFICTION NETWORK
FREE! ONLINE NONFICTION RESOURCES

To learn more about Angie Bastian, visit **abdobooklinks.com**. These links are routinely monitored and updated to provide the most current information available.

Index